Always *With* Me

MOSES MACIAS

ISBN 978-1-64515-067-1 (paperback)
ISBN 978-1-64515-069-5 (digital)

Christian Faith Publishing, Inc.
832 Park Avenue
Meadville, PA 16335
www.christianfaithpublishing.com

Printed in the United States of America

CONTENTS

CHAPTER 1

A Mistake?

The day I was born was the day I was supposed to die.

When I was younger, I always thought I was born as a mistake. I thought God screwed up with me. What cemented me with this idea was when, as a teenager, I had an appointment with a doctor who specialized in genes. He told me the statistics of being born with spina bifida and cleft lip. I don't remember the exact numbers he told me, but he was basically telling me that it was rare and getting even more having both. He didn't tell me I was a mistake, but, with this newfound knowledge and me thinking I was born a mistake, I walked out the office believing I had no purpose in life and that I needed to be fixed in order to have a purpose.

It was July 14, 1988, at 8:45 p.m. I was born unto this world with a *bang*! My parents had no idea that their lives were going to change, but sometimes what you have planned in your life and what God has planned for you were two separate things.

At that time, the doctors were busy so the hospital had few nurses to deliver me. It was supposed to be a happy day for my parents but ended being a day they would never forget.

To this day, they get emotional talking about what happened to me.

When the nurses first looked at me, they were shocked because of my face. My lip was split open and my nose was disfigured. I was born with cleft lip, and it would later leave me with mental insecurities in life as I grew up. Although most of the nurses were in shock, one nurse told them not to get panic and told them what I had.

It was until they noticed that the nurse was holding me with black blood dripping down her arm. She turned me over and saw a black opening at my back. They immediately called for an incubator and put me in it. After that, they took me off to one of the doctors. That later, they told my parents that I was born with spina bifida. My mom never held me that day but saw me in the incubator and saw them rush me away. She would be alone for two hours in shock until they finally came to visit her to see how she was doing.

A doctor finally called my mom and informed her of what I had. They also told her that I would have surgery on my back.

A little after midnight that day, the doctors put my bladder that was sticking out on my back and everything else that needed to be fixed back in place and closed it up. The surgery was done at another hospital called Valley Children's Hospital. My mom didn't leave the hospital until the third day where she finally had the chance to see me at the Valley Children's Hospital in Fresno, California. I was covered in tubes all around my body.

For a few days, I had to get shots about every fifteen minutes. Four days later, I had surgery on my head and chest to put a shunt on my head to drain the fluid going to my brain.

On the first week of my life, I had two lives and death surgeries.

Eighteen days after I was born, my mom was finally able to hold me and take me home. I personally believe that this was why I had problems being affectionate with people until I became an adult.

A week later after my mom took me home was the realities of my condition began to settle in. My mom took me to have a checkup with the doctor. The doctor told my mom that I was supposed to die the night I was born and that I wouldn't live past ten years old. The doctor then tried to convince my mom to give me up to a hospital so they could take care of me. At that time, this doctor, or doctors in general, didn't believe that Mexicans could take care disabled children. My mom was angry and walked out the hospital refusing to give me up.

A week later, she received a letter stating that that particular doctor was no longer going to be my doctor. The nurses didn't know what happened but said that he just left. Who knows what was going on inside that doctor's head after my mom left the room that day?

My mom would learn from those couple of weeks and later that I wasn't going to walk or I wouldn't be able to speak properly, or at all, and that I was going to be mentally slow.

For ten years every day, my mom would pray to God to not take me. It wasn't until the tenth year in a church, she said no to fear that I would die at a young age. She never worried about it again.

My dad handled everything differently than my mom. When the doctors told him all the possible outcomes, he was skeptical. He stayed more focused on the positive things and would continue to live one day at a time with me.

Four months later after I was born, I finally had surgery to take the first step of fixing my cleft lip. As a child, I had struggle fighting with ear infections and bladder infections due to my birth defects. Little did we know, this was just the beginning of a long journey.

Mistake?

Lord, why am I here? Every day I live in fear. You need to take me back because of all the things I lack. What good am I? I'm just waiting here to die. Every night, I cry and ask why? Who am I? How long must I pretend to be happy and live a lie? It's when I'm the most afraid, you remind me that I was fearfully and wonderfully made. God makes no mistakes but made me so. All could see is his glory!

CHAPTER 2

Skate by Faith

From 1988 to 1995, I continued to have multiple surgeries and fought the infections.

Life was a struggle for my parents. My mom continued to do physical therapy every day with me.

It can be hard to see what God has for you when you're in the middle of a storm.

Even though my mom wasn't sure if I was going to walk, she continued faithfully to work on me with the physical therapy, not knowing the result.

Dealing with my condition was tough, but she was getting tired of life. She was tired of the drinking lifestyle and wanted a change.

In 1993, she gave her life to the Lord which would later have an impact in my life as I grew up. My dad, months later, also gave his life to do the Lord. He saw the changes in my mom and loved what he saw but tried to make it harder for my mom to go to church even though he loved the changes in her.

At that time, Benny Hinn Crusades went on, and my mom wanted to go because they were praying healings for kids. My dad agreed to go to help my mom. They asked to take all the disabled children to the front so my dad did. My dad was hungover before the service started because he was nervous and planned to drink while at the crusade.

As he was up there, Benny Hinn went to every child and touched them on the head.

While doing this, my dad was talking to God saying, "If you are real, take away this alcoholism away from me because he couldn't shake it off."

After Benny Hinn touched my head and walked passed us my dad walked away thinking he tried, and it didn't work.

On his third step, he said he felt a mighty rushing wind go through his body and cleansed him out. He went there from being hungover to sober and gave his life to the Lord.

Many times, miracles and healings come in small steps. We often overlook all the little steps that took us at the end of the road.

When I was three, the doctors put braces on my feet to help me stand or walk even if I tried.

When I was four, they gave me a walker to further help me stand, but, according to my mom, I just wanted to get rid of the walker and fought to wear the braces. At some point, I even took my older sister's mermaid skates and used them to crawl around the house. I would wait until she finished using them and then slipped my little hands in them and used them to crawl. At first, I dragged my legs. Next I got my legs up more like a normal crawling position. Finally, I was on my tippy-toes crawling all over the place. Eventually my mom saw me crawling toward the couch and parked the skates like a car, and I held on the couch and stood up. From there, I walked from one side of the couch back to the skates. I did this for about a year and half until I had the strength to stand on my own and just walk a little. It was, at this point, the doctors decided to have surgery on my spine and feet to help me on my journey. I always tripped with my feet but would get back up and continue to walk again.

Valley Children's Hospital, when I was four years old, thought it was a good idea for me to go to school. It would help me out so I went to Powers-Ginsburg Elementary Charter where they accepted disabled kids, and they also had facilities for the physical therapy.

By the time I was six, someone at the school realized that I was not slow and moved me to the school for normal kids. My parents recalled, at this point, that it was like a light bulb switch that had turned on in my head, and I worked my way up to the advance classes. They believed I was acting like the other kids because I was always surrounded by them, but that was not what my mental capabilities were. They figured out that my physical problems were just from the lower half of my body.

I recall that I was being unhappy about my new location because, now that I was with normal kids, I stood out and began to be made fun. It was, at this point, that I realized at around seven years old that I was not normal and would begin to be miserable in life.

Skate by Faith

Lord, I'm tired of the dirt in my face as I crawl through life caring all this hurt. It makes me want to go back to the world as I and the devil flirt. I'm so weak. I can't even stand on my own two feet. All I do is cry and weep. Eventually, I begin to pray, and your face I begin to seek. It's, at that moment in the dark, you pick me up, dust me off, and encourage me to walk by faith and not by sight. We can't always see what God has for us, but we must still follow the light.

CHAPTER 3

Lost Childhood

I lost my childhood in the second grade. It was a terrible thing for a child to go through. It was not for someone to take.

When I was young, I used to have catheter to prevent urine infections. They got a catheter to lubricate and put it on my private area to help me urinate. I did not like it because it was uncomfortable.

I went to the nurse every day during school to have this thing done. I had the same nurse I was comfortable with for a couple of years now.

One day, the school got a new nurse, and, at first, everything was fine. She was nice to talk to, but everything changed one day. I didn't know if she was having a bad day or what was going on in her head.

She had done the normal procedure of catheterization, but for whatever reason, this time, I didn't urinate anything which happened every now and then. She decided to use the same catheter and shove it up to my private area instead of getting a new lubricated catheter. She even did if for the third time. It was so painful inside me not just physically. I remembered feeling so numb that I lost something. I didn't know what to say so I just laid there. She was upset to me so she sent me to my class. It was a very painful, lonely, confusing, and long walk. I was angry.

I later told my parents and she was fired from the school, but I was so guarded after that. I refused to be catheterized after that, except for surgery. I would rather deal with the pain of a urine infection than to go through that again.

It was not the last time I was medically abused. Nurses shoved needles and tubes in and out of my body; doctors used my body to their further career. I was mocked and physically abused from time to time. My heart became like a stone to survive.

I trained my mind to not feel pain and suck it up. I never got the chance to release all the pain and trauma I was going through.

Outside the hospital, I also got picked on. When I was a baby, a woman asked my tía if my parents were going to keep me. She told my tía that I looked like a monster. She wasn't the only one. People would just stare at my face and tell me I was ugly.

On a good day, they would, at least, ask why my face was disfigured. I grew up thinking I was ugly. It was bad enough to feel that inside because of all my medical abuse. My hate inside just got bigger to the point where I had self-hate. When you hate yourself, you hate the world around you. I just got tired of it one day.

I was about eight years old when I got a sharp object and just stabbed myself on the left side of my face. What an extra scar. I was ugly, anyway, plus I hated myself.

I stopped when I notice there was too much blood so I cleaned up the mess. I still had the scars until this day that reminded me that everything that happened was real and not a nightmare.

You have no idea how much pain you can cause someone with your words. I would later retaliate by saying hurtful things I can't take from people.

I also developed bad attitude and fought people out of anger.

When I see how nice disabled people are treated nowadays, it amazes me. It is a wonderful thing to see, and I'm glad the world for newly born disabled children won't have to go through some of the things I went through.

Lost Childhood

Lord, I have lost my childhood deep in the heart of the woods. Man took it from me for all to see. I feel angry and ugly inside as I am forced to put my pain aside. Am I to blame for my shame? I want vengeance, not repentance. Will this pain ever go away or is it here to stay? Although I lost my childhood, it was restored when I became a child of God!

CHAPTER 4

New Friends

After each surgery, I immediately heard a *beep* sound that came from the monitor machine. To my disappointment, it meant that I survived the surgery and was still alive. From my room, not only I could hear my monitor all day but occasionally the other patients as well, if it was quiet enough. I called the other patients in the same area as my *friends*.

If you get well enough, you can meet with the other patients in the playroom and have a decent time together.

About nine to twelve years old, I noticed something about the kids around me. Every now and then, my friends' monitors would not beep normally. It would go flatline or it would give a warning to the nurses. I would hear commotion in a room with one of my friends. I always wondered what happened to them. Did they live or die? All I know was that sometimes I would go by during the day and the same kid was still there; but every now and then, there would be someone different in the room.

I always found it odd when it happened early in the morning or late at night when one patient was traded with another. Check out time for me was always in the afternoon. When I would see a new patient randomly replaced one of my friends, I thought, *Oh, I have a new friend.*

In the hospital, I had a lot of new friends.

This just didn't only happen in the surgery room but also in the waiting rooms. The hospital had its setup so that the same type of patients would all have appointments in the same rooms. If you had something wrong with your leg, then you would be grouped with other kids with similar conditions.

But since I had many medical problems, I was grouped with different group of kids. The two that stood out were when I was grouped with kids that had something wrong with their brain or with their face.

You would meet kids with many severe disabilities. You would essentially grow up with the same group of kids and see each occasionally in different appointments.

There was one appointment that was really important. Twice a year, you would see a group of doctors. You couldn't miss it because it was very important! You would see the same kids every year and see how they were doing.

As I got older, every year, one or two kids won't show up to the yearly meetings. You would hope to see them next appointment, but they didn't show up again. I later found out that few of them died. I didn't know what happened to the others. They could be moved to another hospital, were not able to go to the doctor anymore, or simply died.

The harsh reality hit me hard when, one year, I went to the yearly memorial at the hospital after my cousin died from cancer. When I looked at all the patients who died that year, I recognized a few faces. I just wanted to throw up.

This eventually caused me to get cutthroat when it comes to choose friends. If you didn't want to be a friend with me, it is fine. You are just one of many who came in and out of my life.

I started to just be with myself. If nobody called me to hang out with them then I would just do my own thing. I didn't see the point of getting to know anybody if they were just going to die. I couldn't see the difference from the patients in the hospital and the people outside the hospital. I even stopped trying to get to know the kids in the hospital. I stopped going to the playroom because I didn't want to play with dead children. You could see it in some of their eyes that they maybe had a year left.

As I got older, it became hard for me to sleep at night. All I could see were dead children in my dreams. They all just stood there and looked at me. I could hear all their screams and crying.

I'd been around with so many kids who were always crying in pain that it never really left me. It took me a long time to find peace. Sometimes I could still see their faces and scars from their recent surgeries, who wanted to play with me.

This left me bitter in life because I wanted to die with them. I felt like I didn't deserve to live while all the kids around me died.

Eventually I was the only teenager in the waiting rooms. As I got older, the kids got younger.

On a rare occasion, I could see someone around my age, but I didn't bother to get to know them. I had enough having new friends. I felt like an old war veteran who went through training and met some brothers in arms who were willing to die for him. As the war began, his comrades began to fall one by one. He was eventually left in charge with a new group of soldiers and got to know them, but they died just like the troops he entered the war on.

At some point, he didn't even bother getting to know them because it was just too painful to go through the process of getting to know someone and then losing them. He couldn't wait until, one day, he would die and reunite with all those he lost during the war.

New Friends

My heart is all alone. It's torn to pieces and needs to be sewn. I'm always on my own. How much longer must I endure the loneliness? God, why do you show me all this friendliness? What do you mean by giving you a try? Are you going to be like the rest and die? You mean, your son already died on the cross, and we'll all meet up at the end? Well, I guess that makes you my new best friend.

CHAPTER 5

Red Shower

When I was about nine years old, I remember taking a shower in the morning like the usual. I closed my eyes to wash the shampoo out of my hair. When I opened my eyes, there was blood all over the shower. I panicked and began to rinse all the blood down the drain along with chunks of meat. I reopened an old wound.

On occasion, I would urinate and poop with blood. I couldn't tell you how much blood I swallowed from time to time. I had also accidentally eaten stitches and dried blood in my mouth. Seeing my spilt blood all over me was something I had to get used to.

What they don't tell you is that the worst part of surgery is the recovery process.

I used to hate surgery the moments before the anesthesia and during the recovery process. The smell of anesthesia after about twelve surgeries didn't sit too well with me. There was just something about the doctor putting the mask on me, counting down from ten to one, and falling asleep before I can get to one.

You just get to see the big white lights as you look up. Everything begins to get blurry and spin into darkness.

They had different flavors, but that made it worse for some reasons so, after a while, I stopped picking flavors. At some point, they gave it to me through the IV. The IV managed to be the worst of all because of the burning pain I could feel all over my body as the anesthesia went through my veins.

On occasion, I dreamed of me waking up during surgery. I don't know if I ever did but, in my dreams, I could hear the machines and knife cutting through my flesh. I could also hear monitor machines at the back as well as people talking over me. Until this day, I hate hearing metal machines going off. It triggers something inside me that I can't explain.

There's one event I knew happened for sure. I woke up earlier than what the nurses expected and went into compulsions. The nurses had to calm me down as I began to fall back to sleep when I was in control of my body again. Not once I remember them mentioning this to my parents. It made me wonder what else happened that I didn't remember.

After you wake up from surgery, everything is so hazy. You can hear your family talking to you, which was comforting. On the first day, you're numb inside and only have to deal with the aftertaste of the anesthesia.

The day before the surgery, I usually wasn't able to eat so, on the day of the surgery, I always got hungry but didn't feel it until after the surgery. It was the day after surgery when I hadn't eaten for three days. The hunger pains got worse. Fortunately, for me, I usually able to eat on the fourth day.

However, in one surgery, I didn't get to eat until the fifth or sixth day. I got so hungry that I tried to eat my arms. I was too weak to bite off a lot of skin, but I was in so much pain because of hunger. They would only allow me to drink water for a couple of days. I used to hate it. On occasion, if nobody was watching, I would try to eat my dried blood and stitches if I could reach my scar.

Once I got home, my life was easy from there. I was able to eat soft foods and I was drugged up until I couldn't feel any pain. I just got out of my mind when it filled with pain medication.

The best part was taking no more IVs. They used to cause my veins with so much pain. It was as if I had internal bruising in my arms.

The scars weren't too bad because the doctors did a good job at keeping them as small as possible. You would get stitches, staples, or sometimes both.

After about two weeks, you have them removed. If you were lucky, you will receive absorbable stitches.

But for me, I didn't care because I was used to the pain of having them removed. I told myself, *I have to be tough.* Any weakness meant death.

Red Shower

I've had enough of always being tough. I've been through so much stuff that my heart has become rough. Was I born to go through so much pain that it's driving me insane? How much more pain must I endure? Will I ever receive a cure? Lord, please hold my hand as I struggle to walk through this painful land. It's in the land of pain I begin to cry out your name. After hearing your words of comfort in my pain, I leave change and never be the same.

CHAPTER 6

Lucky Ones

B y eleven years old, I was an old man in the hospital. I remember going to an appointment waiting to see the doctor. The doctor was a little more excited than the usual to see me that morning.

She asked me, "Could I see another patient of hers?"

I said yes because it was the least I could do for her. She had saved my life countless times.

The patient was about to have a dangerous surgery. She wanted to show the parents and this young patient that everything was going to be okay.

When I walked into the room, I became shy and didn't say anything. To the parents though to see me alive and well was more than enough to let their child have the surgery.

I had always heard in church that "Too much is given, much is required."

As I got older, I became an inspiration to people, and I couldn't understand why. Even though I was treated badly, few people saw me differently as I grew up. When I was a baby, my parents talked with other parents who went through the exact same situation. They would show them my pictures of before and after surgery. For me, it was always weird that I was used as an example in and out of the hospital.

Kids with birth defects and disabilities looked at me with respect and looked up to me. I didn't want any part of this because, for me, I was just surviving. What was so special about that?

At some point, even grown-ups and nondisabled people looked up to me as inspiration. It was such an odd thing and a sign of change. A lot of people were being more informative when it came to disabled children. There were cancer movements, autism awareness movements, and other disability rights movements. This sudden shift of how disabled children were treated was something I had to get used to.

From monster to hero messed up my mind. I fought it and didn't want much to do with it. If there was a child with special needs, my parents would happily tell my story, and I could see how my parents looked at me and teared with joy.

The doctors also did the same thing.

I was a poster child who is a disabled child with proper treatment. I was really good with all my treatment and physical therapy. On top of that, a lot of my procedures and surgeries were known to the medical field, but very little was known when it came to long-term effects and success. I was one of the very few children the doctors used as an example.

I had a success story on the outside but not on the inside. I still had so many questions about why I was going through with what I was enduring in life. It was hard for me to stand tall among the chaos and be strong.

Even though I didn't want anything to do with my life and with disabled children, I still allowed myself to be an example. Part of it was okay so they could have something that I didn't have like the insurance. They said that everything was going to be okay.

There were no older patients I could talk to about my issues who could understand.

Growing up was like being a pathfinder when it came to kids with disabilities. I had to go to places no one had ever gone to and created a path for others to walk.

The steps I took could determine if the others got lost or found their way out. I had to show that, even you underwent surgeries, you could still be successful in school. I had to show that eating healthy and sticking to your physical therapy were like. I had to show that the surgeries and procedures weren't that bad. It was a heavy burden to bear at a young age. I couldn't understand why I had to do this but did it anyway. I didn't mind when my doctor had asked me to do it.

Later as I got old enough to leave the hospital at twenty-one years old, she would smile at me and say, "I was one of the lucky ones."

Lucky Ones

Lord, why must I be the one to lead? I'm a bad seed. You can choose another person to find the way. I'll just lead these people astray. When I'm tired and lost, I begin to sit there and pray. Lord, show me the way! I'll only follow you to find a way out no matter how many times I scream and shout. When you lead me out of this wilderness of bitterness, I'll give you all the praises as my hands begin to raise. It's because of you, Lord. I'm not a lucky one but a blessed son.

CHAPTER 7

Addiction

During the second grade, I was sitting in class when I heard my name on the announcement. The person speaking said, "I had won an art contest" and "Go, collect your prize." It was the second art contest I won. The odd thing was I even vaguely remembered my drawing of these images. They were very abstract and wonderful, but I just couldn't recall the drawings. It was more like I was watching myself drawing them in my memory.

I also had chunks of my memory missing. But I later realized it was all the pills I took. I was addicted to all the drugs that were given to me when I was twelve.

Being addicted to morphine and painkillers were a terrible thing. It was like your body needed it to feel better. I didn't want to take the pills, but I could feel my body craving pills. I took more pills than I was supposed to. I even had my favorite pills like having a favorite meal.

Since I had a disability, I had access to all the painkillers I wanted. I took some because I thought they tasted good. I took other because of how they made me feel inside. However, for every high feeling, there was low. These lows happened when I thought of committing suicide and began to think bad thoughts. It was scary sometimes when you do things while high with pills. You would regret it later on, but you could not take back on what you did or said. It was a bad place.

When it came to my medical problems, some doctors would depend with the pills. It made me feel like a drug addict. But the pills won't even solve the problem and made it worse. I had so many doctors, but they were all recommending something different. I got a lot of problems that were easily fixed by surgery and diet instead of pills.

Until this day, I don't know how I ever passed all my classes in school. I came to my class so high, and I couldn't even focus. I was always sleepy and had memory loss for a few months unless someone brought it all back for me. I even hallucinate every now and then, feeling like there were creatures talking to me. It was the craziest experiences those times.

I was no different from a drug addict on the street. We both took pills to get high. I had winged off most of the pills when I was fifteen and went cold turkey when I turned eighteen years old.

It was a struggle, but God got me through it.

Addiction

This pill makes me feel ill. I can't stop taking this drug, and now I'm passed out on this rug. When I get up, hours later, I can feel my emptiness become greater. When will this cycle ever end? Is this pill my only friend? I rest my head on my pillow crying because I can't quit. I'm too tired to even sit. I want my life to come to an end. Saying anything else would just be a pretend. It's in those lows the Lord carries me away from the affliction of addiction and into his divine protection. He cleans me inside out from a drug addict to a new creation made in his image.

CHAPTER 8

Institutionalized

G rowing up heading the hospital have been a schedule to me. You have to be in the hospital at a certain time. Once you get there, you have to check in.

After checking in, you have to wait until they call you. Once you're in your room then you have to wait for the doctor. It was a very tight schedule, and it would extend outside the hospital. I had to eat certain things or else I would pay for it when it came to my health.

I didn't always follow the rules, but, for the most part, I did. For me, growing up was all about rules and time management. I never had any freedom to do what I really wanted in life. I had become institutionalized.

When you grow up under strict rules, it can be frustrating when it comes to other people. I couldn't relate to anyone because they were living under a different set of rules in life.

I decided to distant myself even further with people because, if I break my rules, being around with them would pay for it medically.

I had medical rituals. I performed them every morning just to get the day started. After that, I took my pills in a certain time and performed other medical treatments throughout the day. Sometimes when I left the hospital, I would leave with pages of instructions of what not to do and eat. Not only was this the case when it came to my health but also when it came to medical insurances. My parents could only make so much money or else I would lose my medical insurance. We could only have so much money in the bank and just so much rules to follow with very little understanding why.

Breaking any rules could mean that you won't receive any medical treatment so you either follow the rules or die due to your medical problems. It was just too much at those times.

Growing up without freedom was so frustrating. The older I became, the more I felt like a robot. I did these things whatever that was programmed for me. I couldn't do what was programmed inside me. If I was commanded to jump, I would say, "How high?" It was hard for me to adapt in life and to just think on my own.

By the time I was in high school, having to follow all these rules caused me to be rebellious in everything. I had no plans of living this robotic lifestyle my whole life. Oddly enough when I left the hospital at twenty-one and had my freedom, I didn't know what to do. Even I was rebellious with my attitude, I still followed some of the rules.

Fear had set in, and I wanted to go back to all the rules because that was all I knew. Freedom was a new territory for me as I became older. I was like a man who served in prison almost all his life. The prison life was all he knew so every time he was about to be released, he would stay in prison a little longer. He was too scared to face to world. All he knew were the prison bars.

Institutionalized

Lord, I'm bound by the sin within. I want to let you in, but I don't know where to begin. This heart of mine has prison bars and prison scars. Lord, will you bail me out? I'm not sure whether to believe or doubt. What do you mean you've paid the price of my freedom so I can join your kingdom? Since I've known the truth, I've been set free to be me!

CHAPTER 9

Depression

I was depressed at the age of thirteen and struggled with it through-out my life. In my whole early teen years, I didn't want to go out-side, but I would rather lie on my bed all day in the dark as I fought the thoughts of suicide and violence. My heart started to become heavy, and I could feel a heavy burden lying on me.

Depression is something to be taken seriously. It's not some-thing you can just shake off. It's more like you have to weather the storm. But just realize that it will come to an end, and you have to hold onto life.

I was glad I had a large family because, even though I wanted to be alone, I never really was.

Having someone there for you is very important when battling depression. Receiving words of encouragement helped a lot, plus having someone there to stick with me.

I was at places where to sit there so sad while everyone else was having fun. I wanted to join with them, but I wasn't able to form an emotional standpoint.

I missed so many things because of my depression. I didn't feel like going out so I missed opportunities. I was at a very dark place in my life, and I couldn't see the light at the end of the tunnel.

The worst part is that you just feel like a burden to everyone else and in your life in general. You think that no one will miss you, and that you're just holding everyone back in life. You tell yourself all these lies, and you just dig yourself an emotional grave.

Having depression is like having a black hole in your heart. It sucks the life out of you. Any light that comes nearby gets sucked in. It consumes all of you into one small point that seems to go on forever and ever. You wonder if there is an end to it and what's on the other side. The black hole in your heart feels heavy and dense. No light shines through you, and anything good in life that falls straight through the black hole will never be seen again.

Depression

In all this madness, all I feel is sadness. All I do is mope around making no sound. I'm surrounded by everybody but still feel like a nobody. I feel the weight of the world on my chest. Oh, how I wish I could get some rest. My oppression is leading me to depression. Lord, come and rescue me from all this sad emotion and mental commotion. It's in pitch-black. I hear a small whisper of your voice that says, "Even in suffering, remember to rejoice for I am with you!"

CHAPTER 10

Codependent

I always relied on someone. We all rely on people, but, for me, it was too extreme.

I began to resent when being helped. It wasn't that I didn't appreciate the people that tried to help me, but I simply had enough. I wanted to prove that I could do things on my own without any help.

I let my pride take over me as I became a teenager. It would be my own demise growing up, but I didn't care because I grew tired of being codependent. It didn't matter if I ignored help that would eventually hurt me. I showed all those who looked down on me and said, "I couldn't do it because I was a cripple" was wrong! Looking back, it was really a wrong attitude.

I was not grateful for the doctors, at a certain point. I didn't realize that they were trying their best to help me, but I didn't listen. I just didn't care. I likely caused myself more harm than good by ignoring their advices at times. I wanted to find my own way of doing things when it came to my medical situations. I always failed because of my pride and would end up having to do what the doctors said in the beginning when it came to certain situations.

You can say, at times, that I made my life harder than when it had to be. Even there were times that I proved the doctors wrong, I had to ask myself, was it worth it? All I wanted was my independence in life and not to rely on everyone all the time. I fell into the pressures of high school. I can see all the high school kids develop their own independence. I just wanted the same thing. I paid dearly for my pride one day.

When I was about twelve, my mom was trying to help me get ready one day, and all I did was to fight her off.

After she got me ready and we drove off, she started to feel pain in her body. We ended up going to the doctor where she suffered from heart problem. I didn't know if I directly caused this, but I was sure it didn't help.

By refusing her help, I put her health in risk. Although I would stick to my pride, after that, I started to listen to my parents without questions. I felt dumb and didn't want to ever cause that pain on a loved one ever again.

When it came to my family, I won't refuse any help all that often after that incident. Everyone else was a different story.

Pride is a terrible thing to carry with you. Even when you think it will help you, it hurts you at the end. It's like gambling, but instead of money, you're gambling your life. You may win a game of cards here and there; the dice may go your way, and you just feel like you're on top of the world. Eventually you get caught up in the moment and don't know when to stop. You go all in and end up losing everything you had won.

The house always wins. My pride came because of being tired of relying on doctors, family, friends, and strangers. Little did I know, they were all angels who God sent to help me with this difficult journey I endured.

Codependent

Lord, I'm grown and can do everything on my own. I rely on me, myself, and I until the day I die. It's no one but me from what I can see. Not two or three but just me. I don't need others nor my sister and brothers. This is my pride and now comes the fall. Here I am the biggest failure of all. Here I thought, "I didn't need anyone." Lord, I'm glad you sent the holy one. He picks me up and doesn't begrudge me nor judge me. He loves me and forgives me! Oh, Lord, I'm glad I can always go to you for help!

CHAPTER 11

Not Going Back

I jogged one day when my heart stopped. I fell to the floor, and I could feel my life fading away from the distance. I was about to die from what I can tell.

As I laid there in peace, my heart started beating again, and I could feel my life rush through me again. All my senses came back to me. I was probably pushing myself too hard as I was working out, but I couldn't help it. I didn't go back to how things used to be, where I could barely use my legs and I wasn't physically healthy. I just didn't want to go back to the hospital and do it all over again.

Having medical failures was common in the hospital. You could see kids leaving the hospital better than when they came. However, a year or two later, they came back with the same problems, and you could see the frustration in their face.

I used to hate this as well. I was stressed about it and have nightmares about it.

I remember, one day in particular, when I couldn't walk anymore. I was walking to class when my hips started to go out, and I could feel weak and a sharp pain. I had to ask assistance to walk to my next class. I was so angry because I struggled my whole life with walking, and now I'm walking fine without pain; I would have to start all over again. I had to go back to the hospital again and address why this was happening to me.

Also I had to go through physical therapy again. I used to hate it so much that I would cry at night just to think I have to do this all over again. The whole experience would cause me to have workout and diet. I would push myself hard because the pain from soreness was different from the pain of medical failure. I just decided I'm not going back again.

This mentality often hurt me more times than not. Medical issues that should have taken care of right away should be avoided. As a result, the situation would get worse than it should have. I walked around in pain knowing I needed to have surgery done to fix a problem but would avoid it until the last minute, almost costing my life at times.

I developed a very deep stubborn attitude toward life because of this. It was very unhealthy for my physical and mind-set, but the thought of going back to the hospital constantly made me frustrate and angry. I was like an athlete who trained day in and day out for one competition. As the competition date came closer, the athlete started to think different outcomes and what he needed to do to make sure that everything went right. When everything seemed to go well and the athlete was confident about the competition, he would receive an injury a day before the event by doing a basic exercise. The amount of disappointment from the injury is far worse than any loss they could receive from the competition. You now have to go back to day one of training and do it all over again.

Not Going Back

Lord, I'm having a panic attack because I refuse to go back. Just as I'm winning, I have to start from the beginning. Lord, what sin did I do for what I'm going through? Lord, having to start all over in life is causing me to have strife. I'm in so much anger that I have go back to day one when the race was almost won. As I sit there in my stubbornness, you remind me to go back to my first love, to renew my mind daily as I meditate on the God above.

CHAPTER 12

Always With Me

Just before my senior year in high school, things were getting real bad inside my heart. I was done with my life, people, and God. I didn't care to live anymore. Life was not worth living, and it was only getting harder. I had been battling with the thoughts of suicide, but it only went to a certain point. Now I set my mind to kill myself to end my misery.

I had so many questions for God: Why I was born a mistake? Why am I monster? Why do people hate me? Why do people make fun of me? Why my body doesn't work normally? Does love exist? When will my pain end? Why is there evil in this world? Who am I? What's my purpose? When will the surgeries stop? Why can't I stop taking pills? When will the thoughts of suicide end? Why am I depressed? Why was I abused? Where are you when I needed you the most?

I decided one night that I was going to kill myself in the morning. I was one to never really pray. This night, however, I said to my first real prayer with all that I had. It wasn't a long prayer or anything fancy. My prayer was simply like this:

> Lord, when I was born, I was handicapped;
> when I go to sleep I'm handicapped; when I wake
> up, I'm handicapped; and I will always be hand-
> icapped. Lord, if I wake up tomorrow and I'm
> not fully healed from this disability, I'm going to
> kill myself.

I cried myself to sleep after that.

The next morning, when I woke up, I was still disabled like I've always been. I thought I gave it my best shot, and here I am still in the same condition.

No one in my family was home that day when I woke up so it made the process even easier. I went to the restroom to do my medical routine crying.

When I was done, I stood in the middle of the restroom thinking about how I was going to kill myself. I first thought to hang myself, but I didn't think I could make a tie strong enough to hold my body weight. Second, I thought about cutting my veins until I bleed out, but I didn't want my family to be traumatized from all the blood when they found my body. Finally, I decided to get my dad's gun and shoot myself in the heart; that was the source of my pain and I wanted it to end.

As I stood there ready to pursue my plans, I heard a voice deep within me saying, "Who are you?" I looked around me to see who said that.

I oddly enough asked, "What do you mean?"

The voice then replied, "Who are you taking a son away from his mother and father? Who are you to take a little brother away from his older sister and brother? Who are you to take away a big brother away from his little brother?"

In shocked again, I asked, "What do you mean?"

The voice replied, "Your mother used to kiss your cuts when you were little, and it used to be enough to make it all better, but today she couldn't kiss away your broken heart and keep you from killing yourself. Your dad is your hero, but today your hero couldn't rescue you from killing yourself. Your older brother and sister used to protect you from the bullies as best as they can, but today they couldn't protect you from yourself. Your little brother looked up to you and you're his hero, but today his hero dies!"

After I heard the voice saying all that, I felt a sharp pain in my heart. It was a greater pain than anything I've ever felt, and it brought me down to my knees! Somehow deep inside, I knew it was God talking to me. I know how crazy it sounds, but I know what I felt and heard.

I bowed down and said, "Lord, what is this feeling in my heart?"

He replied, "That's the pain your family is going to feel when they find your body. That is the pain of abandonment and wonder all their life why you killed yourself."

I suddenly could hear quietly Isaiah 40:31, "But those who hope in the Lord will renew their strength. They will soar on wings like eagles. They run and not grow weary. They will walk and not be faint." These words I heard before suddenly gave me strength and hope that I never had before. I also remember hearing the Sinner's Prayer in church that I never accepted nor believed in.

I said, "Lord, I'll believe in you and repent my sins. I'll follow you and have faith in you, but you have to be with me."

After that, it was like I was back on earth, and time started to work normally. I felt something come inside me and clean me out. I was a new person and empowered by the Holy Spirit!

For the first time in a long time, I was happy, and all my pain went away. I felt so clean inside. I accepted Jesus in my heart and became a born-again Christian.

I left my house wanting to tell someone what I had just experienced. I ended up walking to the closest church next to my house and decided to attend there.

A few years later, I studied my Bible. I was reading Joshua 1:9, "Have I not commanded you? Be strong and courageous. Do not be afraid, do not be discouraged for the Lord your God will be with you wherever you go."

After reading that, God reminded me of the day I accepted him as my Lord and Savior. He also reminded me of my prayer I meant with all my heart before my suicide attempt. He showed to me in my heart, although I was looking for a physical healing that I really needed. Although when I was born, I was handicapped; when I go to sleep, I'm handicapped; when I wake up, I'm handicapped; and I will always be handicapped as long as I live. He reminded me that when I was born, he was with me; when I go to sleep he, is with me; when I wake up, he is with me; and as long as I live, he is always with me!

Always With Me

*I once wanted suicide until I received the one that was cru-
cified. I used to be lame until I was healed in Jesus's name.
I battled with depression until I became God's possession.
I used to have bad behavior until I received the Savior.
No longer the days of feeling all alone and having a heart
of stone. Now that I realize the Lord is always with me!*

M oses Macias was born with spina bifida and cleft lip as a child. At a young age, he had to endure dozens of surgeries throughout his life. He was always on the verge of death as he had to fight for his life due to the two severe disorders he was born with. As he grew up, he had to deal with hardship that comes with being born disabled. He would struggle with depression, drug addictions, suicide, sexual abuse, medical abuse, and the physical pain that comes with surgeries. Despite all the hardship, he would find comfort in God and surrender his life to Jesus Christ his Lord and Savior.

CPSIA information can be obtained
at www.ICGtesting.com
Printed in the USA
LVHW030200300719
625828LV00003B/395